I0753293

Marijuana Sounds
&
I'm Procrastinating

A Collection of Poems

By

Morgan 'Morgz' Suszek

ISBN: 979-8-9910346-0-9

Cover Art by **V.R. Cherrette**
Edited by **Ramona Suszek** & **V.R. Cherrette**

Printed by **Retro Morgue Media**
Alpena, MI 49707

For more information contact morgansuszek@gmail.com

Author Notes

The blind faith I have in my creative works is intoxicating. With that in mind, I wanted to take a moment to address all those reading this who are enabling that feeling and tell you how deeply grateful I am. There is no high quite like one attained by radical dreaming and with the support of people like you, I now reach those heights.

I have always wanted to write a book. Of course, if you had told me years ago that my first one would be a collection of poems, I would've laughed. Poetry and not the next best-selling fantasy novel?!? Well, it's true.

There was no shortage of support in my corner. The amazing network of friends and family I have surrounding me is unmatched. In fact, I could spend an entire books worth of pages naming names. I won't do that, though.

I will, however, take a moment to recognize the few people that really did drive this project. Mitchel, Dom and The Poetics Lab get the first nod. Thank you for the inspiration and showing a starving artist that pursuing creative avenues like this are possible wherever you are. Nycki.C gets the second nod. Thank you for being so brave and going through this process first so you could share your knowledge with me.

If I didn't mention you and you think I should have, please know that you're in my thoughts. If we are close in any way, know that I appreciate you. I wouldn't have made it to this point without every single one of you, I just don't have enough space to give each of you the appreciation you deserve. Thank you so much.

Dedication

To everyone that told me I could.

Humble Beginnings

So, what's the point?
Still sitting here
Stuck staring where the blank spaces seem to hide
Beyond the line of sight, just right
So as not to draw attention
The mere mention of an opus
Narcissistic, obviously
But even genius started somewhere
Humble beginnings once scribblings from an acid aftershock
Dripping endlessly, stemming and spreading
But I keep forgetting to write them down
Just the reverberating sound remains
The numb foot, pins and needle pains, excruciating
Nothing of meaning is left, bereft
I scrawl and scratch hoping something will come of that
But the words seem too familiar, fall flat
Like they're quoted from another
I wonder if I have affected the sentiments of a different author
Plagiarized pages I don't even remember
I try to surrender to my narrative
Plunge into perspectives that give new outlook to character
A viewpoint that's fresh, not done to death
But everything seems the same through these sights
Taking aim as these thoughts take flight
Too fleeting to take a shot and I only got a glimpse
Unsure of how this all fits together
Re-reading to correct my letters, but something's still missing
A point worth addressing, the morals of my stressing
My writing, my curse and my blessing emotionally
Takes everything but the need
To take these feelings out of me
Without it I am nothing, but with it I am free

A rigid dichotomy
I gladly rest my laurels between
Sight unseen
Eagerly I express until my inner mess starts to decompress
If I can inspire that in even one other person
My life will have had a good enough reason
A validation of what I believe in
A true meaning
Which takes me back to the beginning
My point
To use the ink in my pen to anoint
Herald the preachers of a new generation
An era of rebirth and rediscovery, not indoctrination
Open minds and hearts
Is where it starts
And where this ends

Taking Notes

It seems to me that in this galaxy
The only thing that's consistent's inconsistency
And it's hard to be anything but a social casualty
And it's just gravity keeping your eyes closed to the tragedy of democracy
So you can just keep on living the fallacy
That we are free from tyranny, combat conformity
Don't cop a plea, that's insanity
Travel a route with a little more integrity
A dash of passion, maybe a touch of apathy
Don't give in to the moral majority
Take a stand, menocide this monopoly
This is what I see, taking notes on reality

Respectfully, be real with me
Let me know if your method isn't honesty
Tastefully, be the king of hypocrisy
So I can stay clear of thee and thy royal company
I don't need the phony
Over-exaggerated, high and mighty
You are the enemy
Draining my energy
And, regretfully, I'm running on empty
Sadly, there's no Plan B
I am not an army
This is what I see, taking notes on reality

Immediately, undo the wizardry
Cast of the puppetry, rewrite mythology
Quickly, we don't have eternity
Remove reluctancy
We are the calvary
Question the audacity of authority

Break down the boundary
Hope, not disparity
Introduce humility to humanity
Embrace possibility
New age outlaw infamy
This is what I see, taking notes on reality

You know that life's not easy
No such thing as equality instantly
With blinders on, you can't see clearly
All I wanna know is, "Can you hear me?"

Composed

I've gone and caught that downward motion
Through this endless ocean of emotion
That's constantly eroding the stone around my heartstrings
Not even the power of music makes me forget
I keep hitting next on the track select
Until the waves turn to static, the white noise fades to black
And I am left erratic as the crashes play it back
I stay deaf in the undertow while my mind is somewhere else
Just a shadow of myself
Drowning, no life ring
Determined and unworthy, I drift in the sea
Stuck riding the storm, decibels beyond me
Always frequenting this frequency
And if I had a sail or an oar
I could never come ashore
The current drags me in reverse and I get stuck repeating
It's exhausting and defeating, but I keep on believing that
Someday my feet will touch the ground
Symphonies will make a sound
The world will finally come around
And maybe, if I'm lucky, my light will be found
But for now I will just hold this note through this 12-bar cell
Wishing well for someone to save me from this hell
But only time will tell how this rhythm will swell
It's already too fast, over-lapped by my past
The beat of the drum sounds more like a run
And I have fear that I will not last
I've taken to melody as remedy
I would like to find harmony, but I will settle for anything
A wake-up call, an answer, maybe just unlock the key
I'm composed
Here I go

Blaming Responsibly

It all starts with an act
One offhanded attack
The only thing left intact is a back against the wall
Someone who worked up the wherewithal to even respond at all
Someone who went out on a limb with a prayer and a whim
Shared an opinion and you make an example out of him?
And the thing that sparked the censorship? Total shit
Then personal conversations turned into a public torture session
Complete regression
Not to mention the lack of tact and respect or the courage to admit it
A full out fear of being direct
Just pick and select the good parts, leave the rest
Then the mindset met retaliation
From a station of self-righteous mediation
From a vigilante for social justice that laughs at intimidation
A silver-tongued warrior with karmic ways and thick skin
That loves the taste of one's own medicine
And how soon the initial sins forgotten
And the victim is born anew
Lashing out because the true leaves them black and blue
And, when it starts to fade, it leaves a yellowish hue
So they retreat and try to delete any memory of honesty
Anything too real to deal with casts a depth
And, if exposed, the shallow can lose their breath
It's a claustrophobic thought
Getting trapped or caught
So they stay hidden, ready or not
There's no accountability
Just envy of reality
The dizzying perception of neutrality
And when someone has the nerve to speak up and out?
Oh the audacity

But tenacity is a specialty of mine
A power, if you will
Something divine
Aged with experience, like a fine wine
One I can employ with ease
That leaves all of these subtleties
That and the knowledge that certain negativities are of my own doing
Makes what I do and say responsibilities, there are no blames
It's a "play no games"
A "no things I can just stow away"
A "no, no, no thank you, not today" mentality
That to most is an unreal rationality
But I will stay a reverie to everyone in need
And with act and deed I will not heed
So, say what you will with your weightless words
And speak as though the hurt you've caused yourself is heard
I hope it reverberates back and reconnects you with Earth
Triggers a quake to rock your fantastic condition
Knock you down a peg, wake you up for a second
If not, I cannot help
For this wisdom dealt requires understanding
And that seems too demanding
No station is above scrutiny
And realization makes you angry
End up threatening an infantry
Like I haven't been here before
I stay ready for war
And we can settle the score if you really want more
An eye for an eye might make the whole world blind
But, if that's how you fight, I am down for mine
I'm used to exposed doubt leading to lashing out
And your kind are not strangers to people like me
But I've accepted my flaws and set myself free
Sorry...not sorry

Treehouse

You initiated an invasion
What cold calculation
What mental manipulation
That would beget such backhanded hypocrisy
As did allow such a space to exist in the first place
But safe is just a word to you
Your cis, hetero life doesn't know what it's like
You do not understand vulnerability
You mock it blatantly with your open support of those that repress
The very thing that threatens, is the very thing you welcomed
And there is clearly no lack of intention
As details so unfathomable to mention we're known
And yet throw to the wayside
Cries of those who felt betrayed, denied
Another mission statement lost in a business proposal
Another broken promise that failed to surprise
Most of us are used to it
The "here, have it for as long as we deem fit"
The "I don't care what you do, I just don't want to see it"
The "I don't believe people like you can be equal to me" bullshit
The little black book that shook you to your core about who I find myself attracted to
The fake friends that smiled in my face
Then cast every vote they could behind my back to take my rights away
The only reason I stand here today is because sometimes I feel like I'm the only one that will say, without a hint of irony, what needs to be said
And I would rather be dead than live with the anger bottled up
All the spite we fight through just to be seen, to be heard
The extremes some of us do for the fleeting feeling that we aren't alone
That someone somewhere has grown through similar issues
And yet, somehow, that means nothing to you
Does your vapid shallow existence not allow you to empathize?

Or do you choose otherwise?
How queer, how bizarre
To see you for who you truly are

<u>Personal</u> <u>Insight</u>

This fucking face
With these off-set, crooked ears
A disgusting visage I use to hide my inner workings
An ugly I have spent my life disguising
Caking make-up on made up hairlines
Portable lenses are less offensive
And yet I have never let it stop me
Because tenacity, obviously
Comfortable with my hate
Doing great, honestly
An unmovable stone structure
That has withstood my own worst
What hurt could you possibly cause
I got up over and over again
After knocking myself down
You have no power over me
I *am* The Goblin King

Dichotomy

It's either smooth sailing or up shit's creek
Staying afloat or six feet deep
There's never any in between
I go from one to the next extreme
Quiet as a mouse or loud as a scream
All revved up or losing steam
I'm soft as satin or hard as nails
The best laid plans or the biggest fails
On the right track or everything derails
I can miss the biggest details
Or perfect it to a tee
When it's good, it's great
But when it's bad, it's worse, you see
Indubitably you wouldn't agree
I understand
I can be a real chicken and a ham
Most days I'm a lion or lamb
It's not like I don't give a damn
I can care so much about a mess
And yet still manage to not invest less
I would be relaxed if I wasn't so stressed
A natural born liar, honest
But I digress
What could I say to make you see my way?
A wandering soul that chose to stay
A deity of night that needs the day
A dancing shadow that relies on light
The peace that comes after a fight
Ignorance is bliss after all, am I right?

Xanadu

My muse got loose again
It was trapped in my pen, sweet seraphim
Solitarily confined to my time
And this tragic rhyme scheme
Once locked up, now it taunts me
"Dig deep!" my inner voice screams
I can find the words even if it's free, I believe
The time caged taught a thing or two
Didn't it?
My sharpened wit, heightened vocabulary
Structure, usage
I'm not useless
Inspiration isn't insipid
After all it is but one small, albeit fun, inspirer
Acquired from an all too real realization
Just an actualization of a memory
Imaginary imagery that I had to experience to create in the first place
Right?
Tonight is a new thought, fraught with unease and uncertainty
Still unclear, an idea begins to form
Unfurling its dreamlike tentacles, it encases my brain like a storm
I am enveloped by possibility
But still no concrete artistry
My mind is a blank canvas, and all the colors are swirling
Curling, they kiss, emitting auras of bliss
A feeling I've felt before, somehow familiar
Like a fundamental tone
Am I doing this alone?
Or has a new muse found a home
I'm reminded of the struggles
The turns and tussles
Did I ever say die?

No! Why would I?
And suddenly the feeling is alive
Flowing through me through story
In all its glory
Wait, was this muse me?
Was I the catalyst to this?
I guess my last mess had an antagonist
Arson that made my heart burn
But now my own lack of creativity
Was exactly what I need
How interesting, indeed
I suppose these ancient deities really can be found in everything

Catastrophic

These last couple of days, a constant rage
Ready to turn the page
But the frustration comes in waves
And waves and waves
Being told how to behave
Like I'm in second grade
Overlooking the progress I've made
So I'll sit and explain myself
But your lack of listening doesn't help
So I bottle it back up, stash it on my inner shelf
Let it choke me later, steal my breath
The death of patience and understanding
Done asking, now demanding
How grand in the scheme of things
The anger disrespect brings
A screaming takes over what sings
Snapping all of my heartstrings
Nerves wound too tight
Nauseous, not alright
I cannot handle tonight
Every other sentence starts a fight
Every bark becomes a bite
But I'm ready to nip back
I've outlined every attack
Greased the track and stacked the deck
End up with my foot on your neck, bet
You haven't seen mad yet
And if you keep pushing, fury is what you'll get
Your mind set is reject
Unable to select anything direct
You dance around dialect
To try to prove a point

But now I'm overly annoyed
Like everything is null and void
Blank frames on burning celluloid
The bombs have already been deployed
And all momentum has been destroyed
There is no getting ahead
Spinning circles 'til I'm dead
I'm exhausted
Barricaded, but still accosted
Feeling like I've lost it
Sinking like bricks in a quicksand pit
Good at getting caught in a bad trip
When it gets slick, I slip, and I tend to lose my grip
Catastrophic
But you don't care about my hurt
You just divert, downsize my worth
Gloss over how I feel
Because that shit's too real
And I shut down, depression
You'd think I would learn my lesson
Cut ties with the exterior stress on me
My mind, my body, my sanity
And, for once, you agree
But you still do nothing

Procrastination Inspiration

I've been procrastinating all week
Well, I mean, I have been busy
Dizzy from the high of doing something with my life
Accomplishing things
So, I guess I've just been putting this off
Let the fact that I'm doing a reading be enough, ut it's not
If I don't create something new, I'll just sit here and stew
About how I never have time for a personal endeavor
How 9 to 5 is ruining my clever
Complain myself into a depression
Because I couldn't sit and write for an hour session
Learned that lesson, make minutes for expression
It will lessen the impact of a harsh reality
Don't become a casualty of society
Let your art set you free, whatever it may be
Take it from me, the commitment is worth it
We all have the ability to directly affect
Use it as a positive, even if it's just for you
Do whatever you need to
Create, don't let the clock keep you down
All it's going to do is come back around
So plant your feet on the ground and focus
Dedicate an hour a day or less, just say yes
Don't let wasted seconds get your best
Because you're too tired or stressed
It doesn't even have to be complete
Start something before you admit defeat
If you don't finish it, you can return periodically
Or just accept and name your masterpiece
Either way, start today, it's your say
As for me, I've come to an end
Stay inspired, my friend

A Message From My Mental State

Recently I've been retreating again
Stuck here a slave, plotting my grave
A solitary quest for nothing left to save
My mind is racing, composure: complacent
Retracing lines I am still erasing
Reeling, not dealing
Unfeeling, not healing
Letting my words do the best of getting
Reliving the guilt, unforgetting, regretting
Then blame with denial, myself on trial
An open/shut case thrown in my own face
The hate, the disappointment, the ambiguous disgrace
Always afraid of living without purpose, dying by the blade
Crushed just beneath the surface, caught in a cascade
A spiral downward, a prayer left unheard
Still caught up in what I have to say, every single word
Mirror image displays of negative ways
Over and over, mimicking replays
Self-doubt, my only solid stance
Always chasing something better left to chance
Never a partner to this dance
Just carousel thinking, back around it goes
The gravity of my thoughts numbs my fingers and toes
But I suppose that's natural for a disaster
A mixed mess master
No one fucks things up faster
Not even these written lines can stay on track anymore
I just babble on paper that fades into vapor
Corrodes every staple
The drought brought on by evaporating shallow thought
May leave one's throat dry
But anxiously asking for water makes you

A selfish egomaniac with a complex or two
But who is counting
I'm still writing
Pencil lead just throwing shades
Shadows throw dark parades
Emotional escapades
My head heaving hand grenades
And I am not okay, alright?
Not today and probably not tonight
I haven't slept yet and it's almost first light
Here I lay, like marching into battle
Face first in a pillow, screaming
My mind just looping endless prattle
Wishing I were dreaming
But instead, I'll just switch gear
Rev back up and disappear
In the mind fog I never fully get clear
Get at me, I'll be here

Lost Me There

I dug a well
So deep it could keep me from feeling
A cylinder of sensory deprivation
I descended to deaden the depression
Met darkness with apprehension
Alone with my mind can be a terrifying time
But the quiet soothed me, a lull so exquisite
Heart beats over rapid breathing seemed to slow the farther I'd go
Down below, under every worry, every woe
How long had the seconds been dripping off of melted clocks
As I watched, just watched the minutes cascade and evaporate
Fading memories of a nameless entity that
In the distance seemed distantly more distant
This was the endless abyss I created
I was separate, it was bliss
For as long as it lasted
Then a realization so cryptic it was almost unrealistic
I once feigned existence and, in those fathoms, I missed it
I had departed from the story I started
Certain characters proved too one-sided
So I removed myself from my own arc
Leaving a plot hole barely large enough to notice
But for me, it was a black hole
Every sordid detail gathered
Every abhorrent villain laid claim to this empty space
But these details can't go untamed
I may be just a footnote, but I control the chapters of this legend
And this is how I chose to defend it
With abandon
I feel safe here, but out there it festers
And the longer I wait, the worse it gets
Hiding isn't very proactive

But my mental state deserves this
I guess both are necessary evils
But I'm exhausted

Disorder

Anxious, ecstatic, overindulgent impulse
Panicked, but my exterior reads false
My heart rate hurries
Inner working worries
The flickers and flutters
Come out in intermittent shakes and shutters
I fumble and fidget
Bumbling with sweaty digits, I nibble at my lips
A thought of biting finger nails
While the butterflies invade my entrails
Stomach floating
Certainty eroding
The energy flowing within me
Sending shock waves through my body
A jolt to my bloodstream leaves me charged and wired
I come off nervous, but, honestly, I'm just weird
The thrill of being here
Almost made me stay clear
But I made it, I'm not afraid
It's just the courage it takes has my thoughts delayed
I am, by my dry mouth, betrayed
And it's not just today, I've done this time and again
You'd think, at some point, I'd get past where the chills begin
But vertigo has got me in a spin
Trying to slow down so I can catch wind
The initial jitters won't leave
I can barely breathe; I scoff and heave for relief
But the stress takes me deeper
The climb out gets steeper
I stay standing, shifting weight
Caught in a debate with myself about how great it would be to go home
Forget whatever it is and just be alone

So yes, maybe anxiety likes to mess with my sanity
Pull my nerves like strings in a symphony
But ultimately, I'm the conductor
Controlling the movements that lie under
The skin I'm in is not so thin
Sometimes a tick can be used to your advantage
And sometimes it pays to be adventurous
Don't let the gravity of society pressure you into anonymity
You have the power to overcome these anxieties
Don't stay trapped and unsure
Be heard, cause a stir
You don't have to live obscure
Getting noticed won't hurt
Getting discovered might work
You'll never know until you try
Don't get caught up with the, "Why?"
You could be going instead of staying
The spotlight is waiting

Space, For You

The stars told me how proud of you they were
A blur of flickering flares like an optical cosmic telegraph
So bright it could bring those faint of sight to see
The pulse of the shock waves enough to bring anyone to their knees
For you
A speck of insignificance existing in limitless independence
The heavens dance for you tonight
I know, they told me
So, however lonely the gravity
The weight of that black hole
Or empty the shades of dark, matter
At least to someone who will listen
When the skies shout praises
Superman
I share your solar nocturne
So you may know its love

I Told Me So

If I told you the thought of you was like heartburn
I know it wouldn't make a difference
It wouldn't stop the yearning
It wouldn't make recompense
It wouldn't silence my regret for not holding you tighter, a chance I don't deserve again
Why did we decide to initiate this moment of weakness
That time you let me see you and you left me in awe of the person I saw
It was so raw and beautiful and the only thing unusual about it
Was why we never explored before
How did we ignore this electric connection
This magnetic direction
This thing that felt like I had somehow touched a reflection
Then light fade into deception anyway
Love just a weapon in the game you play
And maybe it was me, I don't know what to say
I'm sorry if that's the case
But even music is losing its taste
I've tried to pretend that you don't ignite the fires in my head
The endless amounts of poetry you inspired, most of which only you have read
If I told you that every time I see you, your glow, no matter how bright, makes me feel less dead
Would it change anything to some form of instead
I think, for you, I could even make amends with playing with imaginary friends
I think I could try to make my feelings ghosts
If it meant getting comfortable with getting close
Maybe compose a little, kind of like we used to, I suppose
Platonic, of course
I mean, I could try, couldn't I?
Tell that voice in my head that wants to scream from the mountains

That maybe, in this case, just this once, it's okay to hang back in the closet
Silence the fountains that spring forth and cascade the truth I wish to share with you
And dry their wading pools until there is nothing but pits
Empty enough to fill with my intents and an apt metaphor for what us now represents
All that and if it meant any time spent within a tangible distance of your body heat
Then I will meet you somewhere even more than halfway between
Whatever you need, please
I am not normally one, but I am begging
Letting my pride stay left in forgetting
Betting my life to live with regretting
As long as you are part of the setting
I could keep my blood from letting me expose my true feelings
Silence the pulse that pounds on
Beating me senseless with a rhythm that is speeding
I could slow my breathing, force this flood fleeting
See, my breath is bated
Maybe it's not that complicated
But I know better

Taken For Granted

Remember that one friend?
What happened?
When did things change, so drastic
Everything that was real, so plastic
There was a point when we were close
But now that person's like a ghost
At most, the living dead
A true zombie, infested
Things said, directly neglected
Picked the poison instead
And I'm left wondering
All the years I've spent struggling but still supporting
Did I do something to deserve the ignoring
Exploring the idea upsets me even more
Because I wasn't told, we don't talk like before
Everything is surface level
And when niceties run out, you bring up the devil
Then the inevitable anger and disappointment
The monetary moments, just apology ointment
But the feelings never died
For a while they'd subside
Hell, I tried
But it hasn't been the same since you lied
The make-up attempts fell flat
Because money never made up for that
And it never seemed sincere
Because I would still have to hear
The details of what happened and, of course, what comes next
My requests get stuck in a soundproof vacuum vortex
Oh the pounding in my cerebral cortex
But even if you heard what I have to say
I would still play the bad guy anyway

Because how could something good be bad
The best good you've ever had
But have you heard what they say about too much
How it can warp your perception, leave you out of touch
Living to get your fix
Like you're fully addicted
But, somehow, I'm the one
By my own vices undone
Too busy to spare time
Unless it's convenient for me and mine
Absent when needed near
Overly-expectant when here
But when support was needed, it was you who wasn't there
See, you can't just pick and choose
If you're too preoccupied with winning, who's left in your corner when you lose
If you're better without, bolder
Then give me back my shoulder
Lean on someone else
I hope it helps
It won't, because you know you're in the wrong
But if you feel it's where you belong
Then, by all means, stay lurking
I can't make you a better person
But my silence sure as hell isn't working

Resolution

I stopped being nice to the people that don't deserve it
No longer a civil servant
I've burned a lot of bridges
Designated conscious decisions
To ease my mind and focus my vision
I got tired of the kind that don't listen
Incessantly repeating until I'm screaming
Vocal chords bleeding
Ignorantly ignoring
Unknowing cannot be excused once told thrice
Say you want wisdom, but what good is my advice
Done with the ones with words without means
Another broken promise is all they'll ever be
Too busy
I cast out those with doubt over what I'm about
And shouted my truth louder to drown their noise
Some treated me like toys, but forgotten and discarded is not the end of my story
I grew above the child's play, went with those that handled more maturely
Surely, it isn't just me
Finally saw through the veil and realized it could be pulled back so easily
Done rolling over for a difference in opinion
When the world we live in is on the brink of oblivion
Idle actions are allowing avarice from a high place
Stuck in a loop, this human rat race
The solution is sustainable
Equity is attainable
Fiscally speaking; we only have one Earth
But that's another rant all together
Let me divert
No longer will I hunch forward for the noses over my shoulder
I'm wiser and older, and maybe I am a bit colder

But I've waged wars with the weather inside me for years and finally I feel bolder
The fire's ablaze, I've burst from my smolder
Not letting anything emotionally impede
It always got my best, unbearable amounts of wasted energy
But I'm standing tall in the wake of it all
Continuing my rise, while the shunned fall
Trying my best to change for the better, be that go-getter
That does what others don't dare
Unafraid to take it there
So bring on the new year, let the cycle start anew
Everything is clearer already, a beautiful view
Breathing more steadily, the weight has lifted
Sharing what I was gifted more consistent without restriction
Staying uplifted and holding my tongue for no dimwitted
Still defiant, just no longer reliant on anyone but myself

Had To Get It Out!

Sometimes, when the emotions get too loud, I write to quiet the crowd
When the commotion cacophony crescendos to a peak
The highest point is too much for me
So I hush the beast
Reluctantly he retreats because my mind is too busy
Calculating sentences while wrapping words make me dizzy
A different degree of inner working
A kind of diverting
Not regression, I keep the aggression
I just dig a deep impression so it stays in one place with my intention
There is no burying
If anything, it brings it to life so it's staring into my eyes, glaring
And I am forced to face my feelings
It's the only healing that's ever helped
No matter what I was dealt this is the way I would sort how I felt
That's the reason I'm here right now
Because I need to calm down and this is the best way I know how
I was crying before this began, a broken man
Now I'm a dozen lines in and I barely remember when
Or why it was worth the tears or the empty fears
Or the worry or the stress or the frustration
But all that temptation
Some drama adds flair and motivation
But results vary and without hesitation can lead to my exact situation
Mixed messages and spaced-out signals can leave a lot of undisclosed details
And trying to fill in the blanks often fails so the conversation derails
And skids off the track until all that's left is wreckage intact
And by then it's too late, there's no turning back
Just one vicious attack after another until we forget why we were fighting
It becomes about hurting the other, spiting
So we speak like our syllables will smother and stun and silence
Offhanded threats of vague violence, left feeling childish

And stupid for saying those dumb things we did
We joke and we kid but we rarely forgive
Endless apologies, we're both unworthy
So here I sit, undeserving of nothing I didn't earn
That's triple negative, three times the burn
Maybe someday I'll learn I can pass on this turn
But for now, I run on instinct, I get where I need
But I'm okay with maintaining this speed until I'm around this bend
Until I truly mend whatever is wrong
Because in this moment I'm thinking of turning this poem into a sad song
And that gives me hope that my heart does go on
If you don't understand, I can't expect you to
But for some reason this is what I do
Because I feel, and I've always been too real to act like bullshit never happened
Sometimes I have my own honor to defend
At the end of the day, I do care, but I'm not afraid to take it there
And this exists so I'm clearly not unaware of the despair
And honestly, I will probably use this to repair the damage
Letting them in might take off the edge, talk them down from that ledge
We all crave release and whatever brings us peace
But sometimes the two things cannot collaborate so easily
And maybe it's selfish the way we do this
But you can't restart until the first try is finished
Communication is key to any relationship
And maybe we can both step back and get a grip
Try again when we're ready to listen
Until then, take care my friend

Let Love

I've been known to hold a grudge
Stand my ground and never budge
Cut ties with lies behind real eyes that don't realize the pain they cause
It all starts with forgiveness
An apology would give this
This mess of stress would digress, put an end to the tension between us
But that never was your way
You push away anyway
To a different day and it's all about you and you just stay
Confident that time spent trying to implement and enforce
Was all well and did tell of the infidel in your midst
But that's just your mind over-working
About a lurking suspicion, rash decision collision
Face to face, no time, just space. But where is Grace?
The bigger person, the one who's certain their not hurting
The being that's screaming to be heard
Do you hear the nothing longing to be made something
It echoes in everything eternally
Deemed worthy, but only if the voids are left empty
Wandering endlessly toward a goal that is fleeting
Meeting at the margin, backspace deleting
And maybe time just flows
And we're forced to see where it goes
But you're here in the present, be present
Enjoy it for a second
Curse or a blessing, it's only worse with the stressing
Let love

An Ode To Pure Michigan

I'm huddled here, warm
As I listen to the storm
Rage on until the morn'
So hastily the freeze
So, throw a log on the fire
As the mounds pile higher
And the landscape grows dire
Snuggle close before you're froze
The snow is drifting
The weather keeps shifting
The wind is whipping
Not stopping, temp dropping
I can almost see my breath
The icy grip of death
No life outside is left
Hibernate while you wait
Water forms crystals
The prickling cold bristles
Long after night chills
Enter the winter
Seasons go and they will come
Steady as a beating drum
Now we're stuck 'til this one's done
The cycle of the Earth's pull
It becomes a slippery slope
You can easily lose hope
Some just can't cope
They go tropic to escape it
The shoveling, the plowing
Time travel allowing
The breeze still howling
Frost covers, shiver shudders

Cloudy, the sky now grays
Darkness falls on shorter days
You can count on the delays
The wonderland at hand
At least the holidays are near
When family and friends are here
Imbibing in the merry cheer
Santa comes, carols sung
Then the icicles stretch forth
As the front moves North
Nature screams for rebirth
The months go on too long
And there isn't any hero
To save us from Sub-Zero
This atmosphere of sorrow
We must endure the arctic air
But every blizzard gets withstood
Every flurry, we're still good
Worth every sled trip from our childhood
Hailed victory over wintery
The polar vortex is too small
To keep us from standing tall
We've been through every squall
No avalanche will move our stance
No amount of sleet
No powder will defeat
Through the slush we'll ski
Again and again, pure Michigan

Burnout

Velvet green with a purplish hue
A poof of contrasting grays to subdue
Any trace of blue in you
The everyday black and white
How dark or bright the light
A kaleidoscope mix and twist
Amber embers kiss my lips
And disappear with a clear wisp
Pale pink, gold crystal sparkle
Spark quick and glass clear marvel
Blind shine all woes
The mellowest of yellows
Even the most common color delivers
Glowing silver slivers
Guaranteed to give you shivers
Orange hairs stand on end
Goosebumps, the smoothest blend
Raised too high to comprehend
Or ever come down again
Just lost in turquoise sky
Pearlescent clouds roll on by
Can't seem to remember why
It took so long for me to fly
But this feeling, like time, dies
The night goes violet
The moon 'a fire, almost violent
But in passing that too drains
Until nothing but charcoal remains
Smeared ash stains
A blackened cosmic canvas

Twirls and drifts
Until it all blurs to mist
The prism spectrum no longer exists
Just endless bliss

Subliminal

My friend introduced me to Mary Jane yesterday
Now my head's all cloudy and I can't get her off my brain
Now the smoke's rollin' in 'cuz the fire's been lit
Looking up from the ground I can't take another hit
Lost in a haze when she showed me her ways
Caught in the blaze I could stay here for days
And fade away
And fade away
And fade away

I got nervous but I worked up the courage to ask for a dance
Green eyes don't be shy, give me just one chance
Much closer now in the blink of an eye
When we hold hands, the sparks start to fly
Heart's beatin' fast, but I know it won't last
I'll spend forever forgetting the past
And fade away
And fade away
And fade away

Baby, I still love you, but now I can't have you around
Things are looking up for me but you and me are going down
Now I can't sleep and my eyes are red
My mouth is dry from words left unsaid
But someday I'll return, and, baby, we'll burn
And fade away
And fade away
And fade away
Baby, we'll burn
And fade away
And fade away

And fade away
Baby, we'll burn

Bad Harvest

I whisper, "bad harvest," in an attempt to mute my excitement
The universe must not hear of my good fortune
For fear that it will steer me toward disappointment
I have grown weary from the stress of trying not to manifest
Lest I invoke the wrath of some Old World God or Goddess
I can barely describe, let alone maintain, the strain
But for now I will take solace in the pain
Use it as a camouflage to cloak from cosmic woes
Blend into the background long enough to impose
My will, which will not be undone by a force unseen
No deity, no high supreme, no king or queen nobility
Karma has its ways and at some point it repays
So maybe I'm past the haze of delays and today is my day
I've been told to actualize but I've come to realize
When left a surprise the outcome satisfies
Plus, the energy that you put out does not always return
At least, not in the sense you yearn for
Nor does it restore the space that power once inhabited
So it's best not to think of it
No dwelling on what could've been done
No praise until the prize is won
Pride can be a dangerous gun
It can kill or stun
Or become a jinx of self-righteousness
Galactic humility taught by the best
So, for now, I will not test
The majesty and prowess
Of forces much greater than myself

EventFall

Evil invades this vile veil, shrouds
Hangs in the black above our beds, inside our heads
It seeps in, pervades, permeates, creeps
Not even the deep of sleep can keep it
But the wicked seems to fit right in
Goes unnoticed, belies and blends
Silently managing its dividends
At length to which its tendrils extend
And oh how they bend
And coil and twist
Not a weakness unexploited or opportunity missed
The poison of its deadly kiss
Burns and infects inner sanctums endless
The toxic fumes slither and wisp
The noxious gas tightens its grip, venomous
The heinous disguised in weakened minds
The extremely enlightened that choose to stay blind
It's hideous how no one notices
All the beauty invaded by ugly
So suddenly, the putrid procession parades past
Watching the wretched
Beyond grasp, but so obvious
Still oblivious
To the acts that have happened
Playing pretend, too tuned out to comprehend
The sinister stay smirking while you fear, ignore and disappear
At even a thought so queer
Some even get angry at weird
So they choose to be anywhere it doesn't interfere
Until it's cured
No compromise, no word contrary is heard
It is the devil holds them silent

Tongues taken from right inside them
And the demon stays free to roam
Invading every house and every home, never alone
Yet we shun the paranoia
To the delusional, it's just another phobia
But maybe it really is that scary
Something lurking around every corner, very hungry
An ancient being awakened when man first made flame
That has slowly claimed revenge from its dark, recessed cage
Awaiting the day the light fades away
And it can regain its throne of shadows
But for now it stalks the death row gallows
And it haunts and preys on the dim and misled
The ones with nightmares that won't leave them
Gruesome visions fill their head
Slowly it lets the madness take hold
A precarious plot, so bold
Recruiting its soldiers the fire spreads and smolders
And it never truly goes out, not as long as there's doubt
And there's never a drought
So stay afraid of great unknowns
Some strangers may have remains locked inside
Bones buried deep like the secrets they hide and keep
And when brought to the surface, exposure can be dangerous
The only painless approach is force it underneath
Below where it cannot fully reach humanity
Don't ignore it, but never give it your energy blatantly
It can sense vulnerability
I can only plead so much
But we're all in this battle, it's your choice to step up
Some of us are already fighting, and we need more than luck

The Stalk King

The Jack-O-Lantern's smile, so wicked, so vile
Set atop the life-like vines, gathered in a pile
From near and far pointed hats gather en mass
As a circle, joined as one, they invoke and cast
Ancient chants that entice the ever wandering souls
Their voices rise as one as the midnight bell tolls
Louder and louder the cacophony crescendos
'Til unison rest least echoes as mementos
Then, no birds or breeze, no noise at all is left
A still that takes away your breath, leaves you cold as death
Suddenly a rumble, a deep down, distant quake
Rushes to the surface as the earth begins to shake
The coven doesn't break away, they just stay unfazed
Steadfast as they hold their ground through the seismic waves
At once it is done and the evening falls silent
The kind that leaves unease because everything's too quiet
And just like that, all around, the ground begins to smoke
Deep within flowered troves, the darkened smog arose
Toward the center Jack it floats, in its eyes, through its nose
All of this, and yet, not a single witch has broke
Many moments pass and the dark clouds subside
Rooted with the pumpkin, something glows from inside
Slight movements start to show, the plants seem to crawl
Coiling and twisting, and then an upward sprawl
A form takes shape, more familiar than most
Something strangely human, but more golem than ghost
There are arms and legs, but three times mans size
And a gourd for a head, with hollowed-out, black eyes
Monstrous and standing tall, awakened by the summoning
Those involved with this spell now open up the ring
They shout and they sing for the vengeance he will bring
Why else, after all, would you ever call upon The Stalk King

The Scariest Nightmare I've Ever Had

I awoke in my bed
The night was dead
I was young, still in my parent's home
They were there, I wasn't alone
That's why I wasn't startled by the distant moan
A few in my family have been known to saw logs
Figured a trip to the bathroom would prove the cause
Down the hall to my parents' door
A peek revealed they were there no more
I stepped in to look around
That's when I saw *him* on the ground
A hulking man with bolts in his neck
Sat erect, looking me direct in the eyes
It was Frankenstein's Monster to my surprise
I retreated to from where I came
Closed the entrance all the same
I thought maybe my brother was to blame
To my left was his door frame
I expected laughter, maybe he would snap a picture
But no sibling, just a man hanging upside down from the light fixture
It was Dracula, his eyes snapped open wide
I panicked, I needed a place to hide
I ran to the bathroom just behind me
There I could lock myself in, at least
But something kept me from following through
A silhouette in the shower, greenish blue
I opened my mouth but the scream wouldn't begin
Then, around the curtain, The Creature stretched a fin
Returning down the hall, toward the back door I ran
But when I peered through the window I could see The Wolf Man
Diverted to the front door on the basement stairs landing
Determined to fight as long as I'm standing

But I froze when I saw outside
In the front yard was Frankenstein's Bride
The basement was the only place left
I turned but The Mummy was on the first step
I was trapped, no way to escape
The over-whelming feeling it's already too late
I bolted back to where I awakened
With a slam I began barricading myself in
A wooden chair, the dresser, the pictures on the wall
Even the clothes in the closet, I piled it all tall
Then I dropped to a crawl, under the mattress
As the sounds hit the door, I couldn't help feeling hopeless
I could hear my window shatter
Shards hit the floor, broke and scattered
I lifted myself up off the carpet
Held myself below the box spring
I'll never forget
My blood beat so loud I couldn't hear a thing
I could see the shadows surround
But still all I heard was the beating pound
I closed my eyes for what came next
Suddenly, The Monster's fist through my chest
I awoke in my bed
Sweaty, face red
Deep breath
It was all in my head

Pagan Mantra

I believe in a spirituality
Like those that came before me
I am in tune with the energy
Forces eternally
Elemental in thought, word and deed
Individuality is our creed
Sharing our power through unity
A one-ness with nature, the core of existence
No resistance, just an eagerness to harness the flow
A persistence to grow with experience
It can be curious
Some of the stories connected with us
Legends with covens of the craft
All the witches wicked wrath
Now some think us psychopath
Forever linked to a contract the devil did draft
But we stay steadfast, practicing our own way
Not a slave to rulers above or below, but we still pray
A spell is just a wish anyway, isn't it?
The hope is the same with eyes closed, clasped fists?
Don't be afraid
It's okay to question how you're told to behave
God was created by man, what we worship has been around much longer
Tangible by hand, the pull of its healing is stronger
It's still something so much greater
And we still return to it later
The never ending circle, infinity
We owe it nothing but respect, it will take what it needs
So remember, always, that you are just a smaller piece
But we all have a place in this galaxy
You don't have to stay scared of reality
There is magic in every seed

Casting Currently

I run my finger along the blade
Cold and calculating
The end of my index finger strikes a pose
As the tip of the knife pirouettes below it like a grim, black swan ballerina
Exhilarating
I feel it pierce, then cut the skin on which it twirled so gracefully
The crimson summoned lazily lubricates the morbid music box I have created
And I am sated by the bloodshed
Albeit my own
The pounding that sounded in my head became a dull hum
And the panic turned to an exultant sigh of relief once punctured
The volume of my exorbitant exhale
Met with the icy clatter of metal upon my hardwood altar
Just a drop was all I needed, my gaze heated
Laser beam focus vision
Driven by an unquenchable thirst for the unknown
The occult has grown ever so inviting
And I have been delighting in ritual
Mind, body and soul
Fascinating
A mere fraction of an ounce of my own essence
Expends enough energies to facilitate the darkest deeds
Like the one I am casting currently
A spell carried out in the name of negativity
Is a curse in reality
Worst wishes on mine enemies
A few ingredients, some whispered maledictions
And then I let the fire in
Flaming effigies steeped in blessings and strange brew
Concocted unpleasantries meant to appease certain forces worth invoking, and do
I feel the shadows pull, see them weave a black so sweet

And all at once the tapestry sinks deep beneath my feet
As I kneel to greet The Old One I beckoned obey me
I contemplate the bargain I wish to make
The give and take that will slake both our thirsts
They want bad if I want worse
Vandalize consecrated ground, defile a church
They don't have to be grand displays
Just participate in their wicked ways
Imbibe in minor violations on holy days
And in exchange, I want my oppressors to know pain
Not just physically, but mentally just the same
I want the farthest reaching receptors in the brain to feel it
Suddenly the spirit
Trapped on this Earthly realm within the pentagram I crudely etched on the floor
The demon did scream and roar
I knelt near the door
The outpour from me of cries and pleas
Led to an agreement of three times three
A body betrayed for each gravesite I desecrate
And with the exchange, a deal was made and the deity did dissipate
I can't wait

Animism

Mother Nature is in danger
And it will be a disaster if we don't change our behavior
The Earth is dying; as the crust crumbles you can't hear the crying
Oh how we scream for green but the powers that be are not listening
Destructive draining, corrosive change
Because we can't accept energy from turbine blades
Or what the sun gives us from cosmic rays
And we should just do what the gas companies say
They need a reason to keep fighting these wars anyway
Some are still in denial and believe it necessary to put the wild on trial
Decide what parts belong to us and divide it accordingly
According to what we see fit to turn a profit
I keep saying we, but I want to say they
But we are the ones standing in our own way
Watching on as they betray
The ground, the sky, the waters
Decimating until desert remains for all our sons and daughters
Next step, the rain forest
Increase commerce, lower oxygen levels
We scream and they ignore us
Increased outrage for the greed driven devils
Driving pipelines through native lands and under Great Lakes sands
Alternatives exist, but wealth demands
And hemp substituting trees
The marijuana stigma, so nobody agrees
They label us hippies, like we're a disease
But our planet deserves better than single use plastic
Nations will drown if we don't do something drastic
Toxic chemical, oil spills
Apologies don't fix what it kills
Yet most still pretend like it's just a test
It's all just fallout, nuclear at best

But our future seems more unclear than the rest
Take action now, what comes next won't allow us to stay silent
If we don't get angry the elements will get violent
Mass extinction reset
Do you get it yet?
We all thought it would end after the sun explodes, eons to go
But it may just be in this lifetime when the ice erodes and everything floats
Renewable energy equals sustainability
What's not to understand, what can the ignorant not see?
We can't keep up what we're doing for eternity
This is literally everything
There is nothing else if we don't all help
One world united
The only option

Sandman

Sleep, it evades me
Those slices of death, how I loathe thee
Stuck in a perpetual daydream
Where the nightmare's reoccurring
Never any REM Zs
Just fantasies of what it might be like to make it through the night
Eyes closed tight 'til morning light
Without my body and thoughts in protest
Anxiety ridden, sweaty, stressed
Tosses and turns
Even the cool side of the pillow burns
My investment sees no returns
Everything still yearns to recharge
But the length is too large
Not enough time for all the hours
But maybe defying preprogrammed patterns is one of my super powers
A prowess for channeling my insomnia
Into formulaic frames of free verse utopian euphoria
Words so spectacular, phrases rarer than nobility
Syllables royally
Dub me the 'Duke of Deprivation'
Like a caped crusader you would put on the stay awake, graveyard station
Whose motivation is to get just enough shut-eye that his eyelids don't twitch
Guaranteed to be up until the day crew comes to switch shifts
What can I say, I was given gifts
I can barely describe my late night bliss
Thankfully there's cannabis
Can I say it?
How it mellows my mood and keeps me motivated
How the stigma is more tired than I and the rationality dated
The few winks I get are easier to take when medicated
I'm better while sedated

And if wearing myself down doesn't do the trick
I should be allowed some form of release without being labeled heretic
I refuse to infuse a pill regimen
Another slave to the food and drug association
I've been told I could condition my habits
But who's to say this isn't already what I practice?
And have since life hit me with a blitz
There's a lot you can miss
Life's too short to snooze through
By all means, grab a few
But stay in tune with what you really want to do
There's a balance
It's not just happen stance
Push yourself, restlessness can be an advantage
And if not, then there's somebody else doing it more right
If you want it, fight
Don't let the bed bugs bite

They Live

Complicated topics: like work
It's just a constant fight
Forever faking I'm alright
Every response comes off contrite
But I still smile out of spite
The customer service, "they're always right," plight
This is how I live my life
Uncertainty in all this strife
Monetary monotony
Stagnant security
Constant scrutiny
Enough to be, but not thrive
Allowed to exist, but never feel alive
So what's the drive?
Motivation lamentation
No spark to start ignition
Ambition, but no burn
Done waiting my turn
Ready to move forward
Break away from the herd
Leave no time to be bored
Mean every single word, not be deterred
But being stirred gets me shaken
The wrong tooks get taken
And I break into indignation
Become another corporate citation
Unworthy of capitalistic crumbs
Take all but his index and thumbs
Hobble him if he runs
Threaten his livelihood, understood?
He should, if he knows what's good for him
Consumerism: the lower end of the spectrum

Doesn't Add Up

The dichotomy of money is an odd conundrum to me
My love don't cost a thing and you can't buy happiness
But they expect a ring and what? Be homeless?
I don't even own and I'm anxious about losing my stake
Accruing interest at a snails' rate
I'm one missed payment away from that red stamped bank statement
Trying so hard to get something that, at the end of the day, doesn't matter
You can't take it with you, and leaving it for others to bicker over, is that better?
If I had enough to stay comfortable, would I be content?
For once cut the loss and see a profit
Would I crave more after over-exposure? I'm unsure
I'd love to find out, see what that life's all about
Procure principle, corral capital
Amass a fortune fanciful
Legal tender, I'd surrender
Gladly give up my guns for some extra funds
Not necessarily the excess, just get what it's like without that lingering doubt
That "how am I going to eat today?"
That "I just re-glued my shoes and still got dues to pay"
That "no vehicle, walk to work because I can't afford the insurance agency"
See? Yet people have the audacity to call me lazy
Because moolah has never meant enough to me
To stay somewhere permanently if said place makes me crazy
It's the ching-ching that keeps you coerced
It comes down to whatever covers the rent
So you take disrespect for a paycheck
Still in debt
To a bank somewhere in the ether monitoring your every spendature
And how you never learn to put that tax return to good use
Loot turns into an excuse
Instant riches become selfish

Just a few things for myself
But it all still means nothing
Dollar bills burn as easy as anything
We stay tired and fighting for a currency we're told we need
Yes indeed, follow the greed
Because the root of all evil doesn't grow on trees
You even require an income to die
Or else it's a Soylent Green, Lovett meat pie situation
You get fed back to the mass market machine and regurgitation
Ahh, wealth, the ultimate worthwhile
Nothing says “up-scale” like going in style
And commerce continues, we live to sell
Wait to think about your sins in hell
But, while you’re alive, do what has to be done
Always go for number one
Waste your thoughts on something greater than a penny
Acquire assets and subtract liability
Claw your way to the top, stay ruthless ‘til you drop
Hero or villain, you'll always be remembered when cash got you covered
Let a piece of paper take control
Go ahead, sign away your soul
If you're nice, you'll get a good price
Besides you've always looked good in green
And you adore that Daddy Warbucks routine
So play mean, get that scratch
Hustle on and off the track
Wake up every morning at 3:00, don't eat
Just purchase and ingest cigarettes and corporate coffee
Run yourself ragged and then come home to sleep
Wake up, repeat
And you too can be happy
For a fee
Sorry, no change

My Rainbow

I've always wanted to share my rainbow
But every time I try, it feels forced
Like there's this remorse for who I used to be
A life long funeral procession living in the wake I created finding myself
That ends up sounding like a tale of caution whenever I retell
So I thought maybe I would impress a little
Deconstruct these thoughts to an abstract level
And paint a picture so vividly
See, subconsciously it began with instability
The inability to reconcile how I feel with the feelings of those around me
Screaming until my face is red and my voice is hoarse
And the sounds are just coarse echoes reverberating inside my head
Every intimate interaction ending in silence that hangs likes the dead
But eventually the hue subdued
An orange that left me energetic
Enthusiastic about an eclectic experience
Embracing the enigma I had every intention of enveloping in love, myself
But there was still a doubt
A yellow I couldn't shake
A fake that took too many lies to make
And any attempt to reconstruct resulted in a break
Too many fissures and the weight can be too much to take
But the opposite still left my smile a frown
A sinking that sticks me to the ground
I have been stuck in the quicksand pit that is denial
It's a trial, but the grass on the other side is so green
A fresh cut smell so strong you can taste it
And the mental stop light illuminates the same
And I finally sped away from all the blue I was living under
And no wonder
The views from other sides showed me the whole spectrum
Separated me from the ho-hum that had become my primary

And suddenly I saw deeper, things like purple broke down
Indigo and violet now
And every shade in between came out
I can see clearly now
The black and white I was told was right
Doesn't make sense now
That I've found
My rainbow

I Have Met Them

Do you know Fate? I have met them
A gnarly harlequin with a two-faced grin
Loose-fit, multi-tone black
Crumpled hat, noose for a necktie
Sharp and focused, like a single edge razor
Unflinching, constant, no remorse
Rapids that demand their course
Fools feign their control
But some things remain beyond us
Some stay out of touch on purpose
For me, it just doesn't add up
Nothing's decided, yet we don't have a choice
What does that mean? It makes no sense
Back and forth rhetoric, intellect or ignorance
All these philosophies make me dizzy
Regurgitated eccentricities
Framed by fortune tellers for a profit
Crystal balls and tea leaves
Rune stones tell broad tales
Tarot cards, Ouija, it's all the same game
But I think it comes down to blame
Inability to grasp reality to some degree
Unable to accept that the person responsible
Is the one that started the problem
A lack of looking in
Some resort to forces beyond them
Personify an abstract idea
So they feel better about whatever
Guilt and shame they can't face
In an imaginary sort of way, but I have met Fate
So, the thought might feel safe
But we'll never escape

Mein

I'm fascinated by fascism
More so by the people who defend but "don't support" the schism
Those that find the ones intolerant of intolerance absolutely intolerable
The ones beyond incorrigible
Taking personal beliefs over facts
In favor of anything that lacks intricacies
In denial of utter atrocities and actual realities
Just picture it, battle lines drawn
On one side, fighting for equality and justice: a veritable rainbow of skin tones, religions and orientations
That prefer peaceful relations but, when pushed, will meet hateful attacks with retaliations
The ones with true righteous indignation that stand together strong against a menace of mainly Caucasian persuasion
The other side, fighting for ignorance and greed: a monochrome palate of white hoods and pale minds
That are fine staying blind to the swastikas on the frontline as long as the Nazi next to them helps fight for their brand of right
You know, the oppressive kind
I'm sorry, Neo-Nazi, I should specify
I'm told the two are different and I don't want to imply
Now that I've said it, though, do you hear how it sounds
Most of the out-there stay steadfast on the grounds
That, "even though it's terrible," they're allowed to be that way
But what would our children say?
Is that how you would teach your child to behave?
If a Hitler youth somehow managed to rise above
Your patriotic duty would be to spread Aryian love?
Diplomatic discrimination
Mass termination
This is where we are as a nation
Ideologies that have already caused so much devastation

Are again gaining steam, this is a very present issue
The ever-growing violence in our society is true
So do you sympathize?
With those who have been held down or the ones doing the holding all their lives?
If I showed my gay pride how quickly would I be denied?
Told my rainbow made someone angry and it's my fault for the hate?
I don't want to start that debate, but I can relate
So many questions, it's overly complex
I try to scream the truth but there's a vacuum in this vex
A wholly unbreakable hex
Arguing with shrunken heads
Until we're dead, lying in our earthly beds
Fate threads torn to shreds
Clueless as to what it takes to solve this
Because the proof just gets dismissed
Does this make any sense?
I even wrote it with a rhyme to appeal to the dense
Trying to build understanding, not a wall, not even a fence
I'm open to opinions, but not when it comes to equality, liberation and basic human decency
This also goes out to anybody that takes the Bible literally
Who teach it as more than just allegory
Who pick and chose the parts that fit their story
Yeah, I'm just as capable to condemn thee if you don't agree
So, do you have the courage or even care to share this?
Spread this post, admit your outrage, make your own video?
The second it falls on deaf ears it will trigger threats like whoa, you can bet
But they haven't been able to keep us down yet

The Trump Impeachment 2019: A Word

It's a beautiful night
One where the political spectrum is angled just right
Where it feels like we're winning the fight
It was proven to be one big lie
A lot of talk, but no real try
At least not for The People, a selfish sort of sly
And then deny, deny, deny
Followed by a refusal to testify
No response to dignify
HA! He just couldn't comply
Because he would never imply
That he's *that* kind of guy
Or him and his cohorts did falsify
He would clearly rather die than reply
Plus there's proof so the bullshit would never solidify
If he aired out that laundry it would never dry
It mattered not, though, for the truth was not shy
It shined through to awe and horrify
Mystify and mortify
And the ignorant did cry
Still with no understanding why
Apparently, now-a-days, the rules don't apply
And a belief is fact through an untrained eye
The thought process similar to fungi
But there is no power from on high
No one at the top that is above the sky
They can hide in the clouds, but we will still fly
Give us a reason and we will unify
So go ahead, glorify and gratify
But we will no longer let him crucify
The name of the office he shouldn't occupy
For which he shouldn't have been allowed to vie

He doesn't even qualify
I pray the time of reckoning is nigh
That there is no one left to buy
And we can finally cut the tie and declassify
This reckless, two-faced Gemini
The new Impeached Alumni
Time to revoke and nullify
Step up and rectify
Modify and certify
And sing this whole mess a lullaby
So long, farewell, goodbye, bye, bye
There will always be a fight
Between what is wrong and what is right
But this is our night

Forgotten Lyrics

I fell asleep on my notebook, crawled between the sheets
And I retreated
To the ghosts that keep me motivated
In the never ending circle, where the powerless meet
There grows a struggle from the burden of sustaining defeat
Persuasive, invasive, in place of something real
Back and forth
Uncaring, of course
Some of those moments, so intense
It makes no sense
And the more they interfere, the more we deplore
But they'll never see it coming, what we have in store
They told us to stand in line, straighten up and you must follow
Until now we fell in place, now that pill's too hard to swallow
Amazing how underlying motive can be ill-disguised contempt
A redefined warning sign
We just got too tired of those long, tall tales
Killing conversations, ruining goodbyes
Controversy over common courtesy
This juggling act on this balance beam
A need to strive for normal, but begging for less formal
All our freedom under their control
I have known the depths of a dark, empty soul
Comatic
Left erratic, but content with the personality I rent
So stint these broken wings and push me to the edge again
I can always cop a plea, convene and rehearse
It's a good excuse to write another verse about this
Serenatious
You know, when the day dies, I feel so alive, it's hard to describe
I've already come too far to stop reaching for the stars
But now night flies, spreads it wings and takes flight

Leading the present into the future
Releasing the suture and letting light bleed through
The tie that binds now just a strand
The time we had has turned to sand
Where will you be when we take a stand?

Vernacular

I've always had a way with words
Nouns and verbs have always served me
In a way I don't think I can ever repay
Every couplet, every stanza
Every duet, every aria
Inspired awe with ease
I aspired a lyrical masterpiece
Well, I still do
Though the past tense applies too
But I don't want to run-on
Maybe a pause in the dialogue...
Listen!
The exclamation brings attention
So many ways of expression
Meter can be poetic
Lend a rhythm iambic
A proper noun so prophetic
Make you rewrite your rhetoric
But I digress
I'm merely trying to impress
With my language prowess
A dialect you can detect
Through descriptive text and intellect
Distract you with my monologue
Soliloquies stenographed, on and on
Am I wrong?
I could stay and play in prose
Notate every detail in a rose
I could scheme in rhymes and comedic times
Chronicle crimes, chase timelines
Hours of for the love of tongue
I think you get where I'm coming from

That's Something

To say I'm humbled by how far I've come
Is a gross understatement
And let me explain
Before it's taken the wrong way
In the first place
I never thought I'd see this age
Living this long was not anticipated
So it might not be to your God
But I am grateful for what I got
Another breath, another day
More time spent with friends and family
Riches and excess
Were never my measurement
And I'm okay with it
It was never the right fit
I tried, believe me I did
Used my youth dry
Never lived, just survived
But lately I've realized
Progress still occurs
On the way to your goals
I'll say it again
My friend
Progress still occurs
On the way to your goals
There is no app for that
No blueprint, no map
Do not live in shadows lent
From others' accomplishments
There it's cold and dark
The feeling of a broken heart
Never good enough taken

All because of expectation
But this is the best I've been
And that's something
Damn it, I'll say it again
That's something
If the choice is lose or win
I refuse to choose
I've been playing the game for years
I'm fine right here
Still moving forward
Still of my word
Never comparing to
What others do
So why start now?
Is my age selling me out?
Drought those seeds of doubt
And lead, don't be led
I'd rather be dead
Did you hear what I said?
Lead, don't be led.

Just Between Us

If you're reading this
Let's keep it between us
This brief respite
Can be our little secret
Like a keepsake
You can keep safe
Under the covers
Between the sheets
Sealed, sheathed
Locked in loose leaf
And even in your dreams
Not a whisper, not a peep

www.ingramcontent.com/pod-product-compliance
Lightning Source LLC
LaVergne TN
LVHW010841120826
845149LV00020B/3433